Fishing on the Bay

By Clem King

On a grey day,
Shea went fishing with Nan.

"I will get eight fish!" said Shea.

“So much rain!” said Nan.

The boat swayed on the bay.

They could see some rays of sun.

An osprey was up in the sky.

"We will stay here," said Nan.

She got a weight on a chain.
It sank into the bay.

“This is the way to get
a fish,” Nan said.
“Put the bait on the line.
Then we wait!”

“When we get a fish,
we must weigh it,” Nan said.
“If it’s too little,
we toss it back.”

Shea felt a pull
on the fishing line.

“Great, I got a fish!” he yelled.

Shea felt the weight of the fish.

"It's a big one!" said Shea.

The big fish swayed on Shea's fishing line.

Screech!

The osprey got the fish by its tail!

“Hey!” Shea called.

“No!” yelled Shea.
“That is my fish!”

But the osprey sped away with the fish in its nails.

“Time to go home,” said Nan.

“Maybe I will get eight fish next time,” said Shea.

CHECKING FOR MEANING

1. Who does Shea go fishing with? *(Literal)*
2. What must Nan and Shea do if they catch a fish that is too small? *(Literal)*
3. Why did Nan drop a weight on a chain into the bay? *(Inferential)*

EXTENDING VOCABULARY

swayed	What is the base of the word *swayed*? What kind of movement is swaying?
weight	What does it mean to weigh something? How is the meaning of *weigh* related to the meaning of *weight*? What is another word in the story that sounds the same as *weight* but is spelled differently?
bait	What is bait used for when you are fishing? What kinds of things could you use as bait?

MOVING BEYOND THE TEXT

1. Have you ever been fishing? Did you catch anything? If you have never been fishing, would you like to? Why?
2. What other activities can people do on a bay or in a boat?
3. Why do you think people like fishing?
4. What are some safety rules that you need to obey when you are around water?

TIME TO WRITE

Write about what the osprey might have done after stealing Shea's fish.

PRACTICE WORDS